Neuschwanstein Linderhof · Herrenchiemsee

Ludwig II His Life and His Castles

Klaus Kienberger

Verlag Wilhelm Kienberger Lechbruck

Castle of Neuschwanstein, built 1869 – 1886, to the left, the Marien Bridge

Palace of Linderhof,
built 1874 – 1878

Palace of
Herrenchiemsee
with Latona Fountain,
built 1878 – 1886

Statue of King Ludwig II by the sculptress Elisabeth Ney in 1870 shows the king at a young age in the robes of the Order of the Knights of George.

Ludwig II Museum Herrenchiemsee

"It is my wish to remain an eternal enigma to myself and to all others…"

Ludwig II 1876 to actress Marie Dahn-Hausmann

Mysterious, legendary, tragic – this is how the Bavarian King Ludwig II is still seen today. "The only true king of this century," as a French writer once said. Ludwig's castles Neuschwanstein, Linderhof and Herrenchiemsee are absolutely inseparable from his very being.
Ludwig's castles are not conceived to be buildings used for court ceremonies to celebrate his royalty or to be residences for a royal family. Having no official function, they are built in the remoteness of mountains and lakes.
They are retreats for a restless, lonely man caught up in his own world of dreams.
The composer Richard Wagner writes, after meeting the Bavarian king for the first time, "He is unfortunately so noble and brilliant, sensitive and magnificent, that I fear that his life must vanish like a fleeting dream in this profane world..."
Only those who try to approach the inner mind of this king can truly understand how his ideas and dreams could be transformed into such unique forms of architecture.

Palace of Nymphenburg, Munich

Otto Ludwig Friedrich Wilhelm is born on 25 August, 1845 in Nymphenburg Palace. The child is called Ludwig as was his grandfather, King Ludwig I. This is the elder Ludwig's express wish. The boy Ludwig is the oldest son of Crown Prince Maximilian II of Bavaria and Marie Friederike of Prussia. Ludwig's brother Otto is born three years later.

The family usually spends the summer at the Castle Hohenschwangau near Füssen in Allgäu. In 1832 Ludwig's father purchases the 12th century medieval castle of the Knights of Schwangau and has the dilapidated castle restored in the New Gothic style.

Crown Prince Ludwig at the age of five.
Watercolor by E. Rietschel, 1850

Ludwig's childhood is overshadowed by his parents' total lack of empathy. After the revolutionary confusion in 1848, his grandfather Ludwig I abdicates the throne, making room for Maximilian II. There is now even less time left for his sons.

Up to his seventh birthday, Ludwig is cared for by Sybilla Meilhaus. Ludwig remains devoted to her his entire life. His next tutor, count Basselet de La Rosée, has a much less favorable influence on him as the count reinforces Ludwig's excessive sense of majesty.

Ludwig (left) with his parents King Maximilian II and Queen Marie, as well as his brother Otto

The education of the two princes is, according to their father's wishes, strict and ascetic. With hard work and meager cost, as well as strict punishment, the father wants to raise his sons to grow up to be conscientious, diligent and hard-working princes. At the age of ten Ludwig's daily lessons already last eight hours.
The crown prince begins to withdraw and to read, especially the works of Schiller, Shakespeare and Richard Wagner.

"My father always looked down upon me. At the most he had only a few cold words to spare for me when passing by."

"I was subject against my will to tactless, heartless teachers. What I was supposed to learn seemed to me be to be silly, boring and of absolutely no value."

Ludwig II at the age of 30 to Austria's Crown Prince Rudolf

The Castle of Hohenschwangau

Mountain hikes and excursions in the countryside leave a great impression on Ludwig. The crown prince, with his vivid imagination, is also deeply moved by the romantic, knightly world of the sagas depicted in the murals in Hohenschwangau.
The swan, which Ludwig's father takes over from the coat of arms of the Knights of Schwangau, can be found everywhere here. Young Ludwig, seeing himself as the successor to the Knights of Schwangau, especially identifies with Lohengrin, the Knight of the Swan. At every meal he takes in the dining room, Ludwig finds these images before him.

In 1861 at the age of 16, Ludwig experiences for the first time Wagner's opera 'Lohengrin' in Munich and is overwhelmed. This world corresponds to his ideas and fantasies much more than his own surroundings where he feels that nobody understands him. The theater and with that Wagner are to become Ludwig's greatest passion.

When coming of age, the crown prince begins to study at the University of Munich. He attends lectures in history, physics, English, French and philosophy.

King Ludwig II of Bavaria in general's uniform and inauguration robes. Painting by Ferdinand Piloty, 1865

*"I was much too young when I became king.
I had just begun to study when I was suddenly pulled
out from that life and put on the throne."*

Ludwig II 1873 to Professor Felix Dahn

When his father, King of Bavaria, unexpectedly dies, Ludwig has to break off his studies at the university and, totally unprepared, is proclaimed king.
The people, however, are delighted with their new ruler. Ludwig, who is tall, slim and elegant with dark wavy hair and blue eyes, soon becomes the darling of the ladies.

Richard Wagner, painting by Franz von Lenbach, 1874

One of the young king's first acts of state is to have his secretary look for Richard Wagner who is penniless and on the run from his creditors. The 51-year-old musical genius will become Ludwig's fatherly friend and Ludwig his lifelong patron. The two of them exchange exuberant letters in which Ludwig writes enthusiastically,

*" My only true, beloved friend,
yours until death."*

Despite his inexperience, Ludwig takes the tasks given to him very seriously. However, he soon realizes that his vision of monarchy – a God-given absolute monarchy – is not compatible with the political realities of the 19th century. Ludwig is a constitutional monarch and is therefore tied to a constitution with little room for decisions of his own. The real political decisions are made by his cabinet and by his ministers.
When in 1866 Ludwig is confronted with Prussia's declaration of war against Austria, Ludwig must, according to Bavaria's

Castle of Hohenschwangau, Tasso Room, king's bedroom

Treaty of Alliance, join sides with Austria. After Prussia's victory, Bavaria is, from this time on, militarily bound to Prussia by an Offensive and Defensive Alliance.

The young king withdraws to Castle Hohenschwangau and has it changed according to his own ideas. Thus, he has the ceiling of the bed chamber painted as heaven with lighted stars.

It is here in this room in 1870 that Ludwig signs the so-called 'Kaiserbrief' or Emperor's Letter after being pressured to do so by his ministers and by public opinion. It is in this letter that King William I is offered the German emperor's crown.

Prussia's Chancellor Bismarck provokes the Franco-Prussian War which ends with Prussia's victory in 1871. According to the Defense Alliance of 1866, Bavaria has to go to war side by side with Prussia against Ludwig's much-beloved France.

The King of Bavaria, who sees himself as an absolute monarch, is now nothing but a puppet on a string.

"I do not want to be only the shadow of a monarch with no sovereign rights."

Castle of Hohenschwangau, Hohenstaufen room, king's dressing room and music room

This loss of sovereignty and the feeling of being a victim of political intrigue cause Ludwig to go into a deep depression. He becomes more and more reclusive and self-centered.

Not for the first time, Ludwig thinks of abdicating. It is Wagner, however, who – not entirely unselfishly – stops him from doing so. The composer visits Ludwig in Hohenschwangau, plays his compositions for Ludwig on the piano and has Lohengrin's 'Morning Call' played by trumpets from the towers of the castle.

To Ludwig's great disappointment, his friend does not stay very long. Wagner's extravagant lifestyle along with his interference with Bavarian politics make

Castle of Hohenschwangau, castle chapel

Castle of Hohenschwangau, Hall of the Knight of the Swan, dining room

it necessary for him to leave Munich in December 1865.

In 1867, following Wagner's recommendation, Ludwig travels to the Wartburg in Thuringia, the original location of 'Tannhäuser'. Consequently, the young king comes up with the idea of building New Castle Hohenschwangau – as Neuschwanstein is called before Ludwig's death.

Castle of Hohenschwangau, Hall of the Heroes

"I am planning to rebuild the old castle ruins of Hohenschwangau near the Pöllat Gorge in the true style of German medieval castles. This spot is one of the most beautiful one can find, sacred and inaccessible.
A worthy temple for the divine friend, source of the world's only true blessing and salvation. Here you will also find reminders of 'Tannhäuser' and 'Lohengrin'. This castle will be in every way more beautiful and more comfortable than the one below in Hohenschwangau."

Ludwig II 1867 to Richard Wagner

Ruins of the two castles, Vorder- und Hinter-hohenschwangau, before 1830

The ruins are located on the hill opposite the Castle of Hohenschwangau at an altitude of 3280 feet and, according to Ludwig, are surrounded by 'celestial air'.
As a child Ludwig often takes walks here with his mother and brother.
The foundation stone is laid in 1869. The blueprint for the castle, a porcelain bust of Ludwig, as well as coins can be found inside the stone.

Plan of Neuschwanstein, Christian Jank, 1869

Following Ludwig's ideas, a stage designer delivers lavishly creative designs which are then worked into blueprint by the architect.

The so-called 'architect painters' accompany the king in all of his construction projects, projects which the king himself plans in great detail.

Neuschwanstein is an impressive construction site. Modern technology such as a steam-powered crane is used. And social security insurance, the first in Bavaria, is set up for the construction workers.

Laying of foundation stone 1869

Stage of construction 1874

Stage of construction 1880

Plan of medieval tower, E. Riedl, 1871

Stage of construction 1886

Records from 1879 and 1880 supply evidence of the enormous amount of building material: 465 tons of marble, 1,500 tons of sandstone, 600 tons of cement, 400,000 bricks and over 70,600 cubic feet of wood for the scaffolding. The construction of the castle causes a flourishing of the trades as never before seen in Bavaria.

In order to be closer to the ongoing construction, Ludwig insists that the red gate-house be finished first and that a small apartment be built in it.

Construction of gate 1873

The upper courtyard is a reference to the second act of the opera 'Lohengrin'. The scene in the opera depicts Elsa and Lohengrin as they move to the chapel in the Castle of Antwerp on their wedding day. Wagner himself provides a sketch of the setting.

After Ludwig's death, the 'Bergfried', a high tower, as well the chapel remain unfinished. Today the ground plan for the tower is marked with flagstones. The imposing Bergfried, at a height of 300 feet, would have completely towered over the existing square tower thus totally changing the appearance of Neuschwanstein as we know it today.

Plan of upper court with medieval tower, Christian Jank, 1869

Top of the staircase. There is a small winding staircase over the date palm leading to the top of the north tower (224 ft).

A wide winding staircase in the tower leads up to the top floor of the castle. As in the Wartburg, a dragon guards the tower. Through a gallery one arrives in the singers' hall, the starting point of Ludwig's concept for Neuschwanstein.

The singers' hall is based on the festival hall in the Wartburg – scene of the legendary singers' competition.

In the beginning, saints or Tannhäuser himself are planned as subjects for the paintings in the hall. However, in the end, Ludwig chooses Parzival, as the story of the grail and the idea of salvation told in this saga become more and more important to the king in later years.

The Holy Grail, a chalice which can bring about miracles, is made out of a gem which fell from Lucifer's crown during his fall from heaven. According to the saga, the blood of Christ was collected in this grail.

Lucifer's Fall from Heaven

Gallery to Singers' Hall

Gallery, Parzival meets a family of pilgrims on Good Friday

Singers' Hall

BEIM · EINSIEDLER · TREVREZENT

Parzival is raised by his mother in seclusion to protect him from the dangers and temptations of knighthood. The young, innocent fool goes out into the world anyway. After he has conquered the Red Knight, he becomes a knight himself. He finally reaches the Castle of the Grail, Montsalvat, of the ailing King Amfortas. Parzival, however, does not ask the king the redeeming question about the reason for the king's suffering. Therefore, Parzival must leave the castle. Later, when he knows the secret of the grail, he can ask Amfortas the decisive question. Parzival himself then becomes King of the Grail.

Following the king's wishes, the singers' arbor is integrated into the festival

King's coat of arms

Parzival's first contact with a knight

Parzival's fight with the Red Knight

hall. It depicts the forest of the magician Klingsor, the arbiter in the singers' competition.

The Bavarian royal coat of arms over the two doors of the hall with the inscription, Ludwig II, King of Bavaria, Count of Palatine, is the only reference to the king. The busts of the king in the entrance to the castle are set up only after his death as the king allows no images of himself in his castles.

Despite the fact that the hall is large enough to hold many people, it is not conceived as a concert hall but rather as monument to medieval times. Concerts are never held here during the king's lifetime and it isn't until 1933 that the hall is used as a concert hall. Now there are yearly concerts in the hall.

Parzival in the Castle of the Grail, Montsalvat

Singers' arbor, Klingsor's magic forest

The Knight of the Swan, Lohengrin, statue atop the king's writing utensils

The Tannhäuser saga, a motive of the singers' hall, also serves as the theme for the king's study on the 3rd floor, here in the Romanesque style.
The king's desk with bronze writing utensils is crowned by a small silver statue of Lohengrin.
Blueprints are stored in the large cupboard under the painting 'Tannhäuser in the Venusberg'. Venusberg is a mythical mountain in Germany.

Study

Tannhäuser succumbs to carnal love in the Venus Grotto. Soon having had enough of feminine charms, he leaves the grotto and takes part in the singers' competition at the Wartburg.
There he allows himself to be carried away and sings a song in praise of Venus and of love which greatly angers the court. In order to obtain forgiveness for his sins, Tannhäuser must now go on a pilgrimage to the Pope who, however, does not grant him forgiveness. Tannhäuser's return to true and spiritual love ends tragically with death.

In line with the Tannhäuser saga, Ludwig orders a small Venus grotto with colored lights to be built next to the study.

Tannhäuser as a penitent before the Pope

Singers' Competition at the Wartburg

Ludwig has a small winter garden built next to the grotto

Grotto

"I was very interested in what you said about women. Rest assured I do not underestimate their worth. However, most young people tend to mix sensuality with their affection for the other sex, and this I do disapprove of. As I am, thank God, innocent in these matters, my admiration for the purity of women is so much the greater."

Ludwig 1865 to Minister von der Pfordten

King Ludwig II and his fiancée, Sophie Charlotte, Duchess in Bavaria, engagement photo, 1867

The tragic fate of Tannhäuser is a reflection of the problems Ludwig also has in human relationships.
Sophie, the younger sister of the Austrian Empress Sissi, shares Ludwig's interest in Wagner's music. On a whimsy and in fear of losing her friendship, Ludwig proposes to Sophie in 1867. After first wedding arrangements have been made, Ludwig breaks the engagement. Ludwig will never marry.
Ludwig writes to Wagner on this subject:

"... luckily have I escaped the treacherous joys of the Venusberg, I am far from my former fiancée Sophie, with whom I would have been miserably and infinitely unhappy. Before me stands the bust of my one true friend whom I shall love until death." (Wagner)

Centerpiece in the dining room, Siegfried fighting the dragon

'The Valley of the Wartburg' and the minnesingers, who celebrate courtly love, also decorate the dining room.

The elaborate bronze statue on the table, 'Siegfried fighting the Dragon', symbolizes the triumph of good over evil and vileness in human nature.

Dining room,
concert of minstrels
below the Wartburg

Six cooks and a chef de cuisine prepare meals with up to 8 courses for the king who most often prefers to eat alone. The kitchen on the ground floor is connected to the dining room by an elevator that serves three floors.

The kitchen is extremely modern for the times with such technical innovations as the free-standing Rumford cooking stove. The roasting spits on the wall are turned by their own heat and the speed of rotation can be controlled by the heat.

The process for making hot water is a great innovation for Ludwig's time. The castle has running water on all floors. The water comes from a source above the castle. There are five large furnaces near the kitchen from which the entire castle can be heated.

Just as technically sophisticated is the electric bell system which is run on batteries. This system calls the servants who can see on a display board from which room the call is coming.

The scullery

Battery-powered bell system

Castle's kitchen

Furthermore, one of the first telephones ever used connects the castle to the village of Hohenschwangau. It runs on batteries and was supplied by Werner von Siemens.

When the king resides in Neuschwanstein about 30 servants serve him. They live in simple rooms with oak wood furniture on the first floor of the castle.
Count von Dürckheim, the king's adjutant, has a room next to Ludwig's study. A close confidant, he remains loyal to Ludwig up to the very end and even wants to flee with the king to Tyrol in order to avoid Ludwig's arrest.

Telephone

Servants' quarters

Count Alfred von Dürckheim-Montmartin, Adjutant

Adjutant's room

Scenes from the saga of Sigurd, the oldest form of the Song of the Nibelungs, are depicted under the massive cross-vaulted ceiling of the entrance halls.
The king sees the tragic heroes of these sagas not only as they appear in Wagner's operas, but also as a symbol of his own personal agonies such as the denial of love, suffering, atonement and redemption.
Ludwig takes over the swan, as a symbol of purity, from the coat of arms of the Knights of Schwangau. This symbolism can be found throughout the castle.

Entrance hall, 3rd floor

"The paintings in the new castle should be according to the sagas and not according to Wagner's directions."

Ludwig to his painters

Sigurd's ride through the tongues of flame

Sigurd kills the dragon

Sigurd's death

Vase in the form of a swan in Nymphenburg porcelain

The saga of Lohengrin with which Ludwig so much identifies is depicted in the living room.

Arriving in a boat pulled by a swan, Lohengrin, son of Parzival, King of the Grail, is sent to the Duchess Elsa as her protector. He conquers Elsa's slanderer and takes her as his wife. However, when she asks him for his name, which she is not allowed to do, a swan appears and takes Lohengrin back to the Castle of the Grail.

By the miracle of the grail, Lohengrin is picked as Elsa's protector

Bookcase

Ludwig knows the libretto by heart. In Lohengrin he sees the incorporation of his ideals – those of pureness and faith combined with supernatural powers.

Lohengrin's farewell

The king, who spends much of his time reading, feels especially comfortable in the 'swan's corner'. However, only a small part of his extensive library would have found room in the bookcase in the living room.

Elsa and Lohengrin with their children

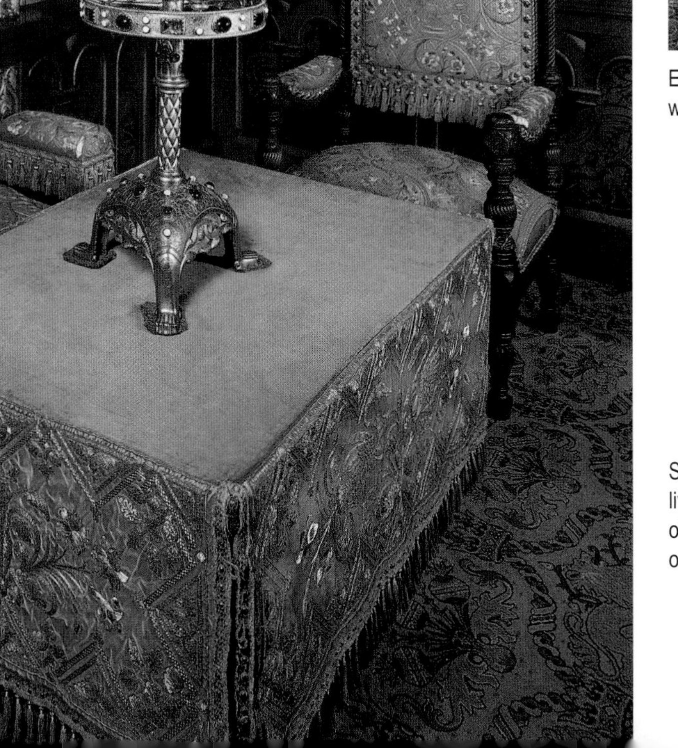

Swan's corner in the living room with one of the few remaining original carpets

Walther rides from castle to castle

Hans Sachs and the meistersingers from Nuremberg

Walther von der Vogelweide, 'I was sitting on a rock.'

The ceiling of the dressing room is the only one in the castle that does not have wooden panels, but is covered by paintings of grape vines. The walls are decorated with scenes from the life of the poet Walther von der Vogelweide.

A curtain with peacocks embroidered in gold on purple silk hangs on the wall. The peacock is, next to the swan, Ludwig's favorite animal.

Hans Sachs, a figure from the 'Die Meistersinger von Nürnberg' is portrayed in the alcove. In 1868 Ludwig and Wagner attend the premiere of the opera in Munich sitting together in the king's loge. Shortly after this, their relationship cools considerably. When Ludwig hears of Wagner's affair with Cosima von Bülow, the wife of the conductor, he is bitterly disappointed.

"In a faraway land, far from where you are, there is a castle which is called Montsalvat, and in the center a temple full of light, so precious as never before seen on earth." Thus begins the story of the Holy Grail. Referring to Neuschwanstein, Ludwig's Montsalvat, the King writes euphorically to Wagner,

"There I can hear in my mind the sacred chants of Montsalvat, there is the place where I feel most at home, at the source, where Parzival was consecrated as king of the only true and real kingdom."

Ludwig II 1877 to Richard Wagner

Originally conceived by Ludwig as a medieval castle with an audience chamber and banquet hall, plans are changed during construction to create instead the Castle of the Grail where the ageing and suffering Amfortas resides. The concept of salvation associated with the Holy Grail becomes more and more important for Ludwig II, also because of his homoerotic inclination which he himself finds sinful.

Throne room

"Whoever beholds the Holy Grail is freed from the power of sin."

Ludwig writes in his diary

The later construction of the Byzantine Hall is only made possible by an elaborate steel construction spanning the hall which is two stories high.
The missing throne is symbolic of Ludwig's fate in that he cannot in reality live the idealized life of an absolute monarch in a kingdom bestowed by the grace of God. The gold and ivory throne was to stand at the top of the white marble stairs. As the throne had not been delivered at the time of the king's death, the order was simply cancelled.

Sketches of the throne

Saint Louis IX of France giving food to the poor

SPIRITUS CONSILII
SPIRITUS INTELLECTUS

Six canonized kings are depicted in the apse. They act as mediators and as shining examples for Ludwig. The apse is crowned by Christ, Mary and John the Baptist. To the left and right of the stairs, the twelve apostles hold the Holy Laws of God. The wall paintings tell the tales of the six canonized kings.

"The decorations of the throne room are entirely the king's own ideas. I had only to look through the plans and to solemnly swear to his secretary that no other person would be able to look at the plans," said an historian who advised Ludwig about the medieval sagas.

A particularly fine piece is the intarsia floor, made from two million mosaic pieces, depicting the terrestrial sphere with all its fauna and flora.

The blue of the dome with the golden stars represents the celestial sphere.

The imposing chandelier in the form of a

Lucifer's Fall from Heaven

The Twelve Apostles

St. George fighting the dragon

Byzantine crown is decorated with glass gems and 96 candles. It represents the royal crown as a mediator between heaven and earth.

In one of the paintings St. George kills the dragon. In the upper left-hand corner of the painting the silhouette of the Castle of Falkenstein can be seen – this was to be Ludwig's fourth castle. It was to be built on a jagged mountain top near Neuschwanstein.

The king would have been able to see the Castle of Falkenstein from the balcony of the throne room.

Marien Bridge over the Pöllat Gorge with waterfall, in the background the mountain Säuling, 6700 feet in altitude

View of Hohenschwangau and Lake Alpsee from the balcony of the throne room

From here Ludwig has a truly royal view of the Tyrolean Mountains, the Castle of Hohenschwangau and Lake Alpsee. Neuschwanstein, located in the middle of a large natural park, is a successful symbiosis of art and nature.

The wild and romantic Pöllat Gorge and the Marien Bridge, named after Ludwig's mother Marie, can be found on the other side of the castle. In 1866 Ludwig has the wooden bridge replaced by a stable iron construction.

Icon of Maria
by J. Frank

Ludwig has a particular fondness for extravagant bedrooms. In contrast to the rest of the castle, the king's apartments are done in the New Gothic style with extensive woodcarving.
The elaborate bed is unusually long for these times as Ludwig, at a height of 6 feet, 4 inches, towers over most of his contemporaries.
The bed, with a relief carving of Christ at the foot end and an icon of Mary at the head, gives the impression of a cathedral. The elaborately carved baldachin over the bed depicts church towers from different German cathedrals and churches.
A swan on the washstand serves as a water faucet.

The Resurrection
of Christ

Washstand

Offering the love potion

The wall paintings depict scenes from 'Tristan and Isolde'. Renunciation of sensual pleasures is the central theme here. The beautiful princess Isolde is to marry King Marke. However, Isolde and Tristan unintentionally drink a love potion and fall madly in love. Isolde marries Marke, but her heart belongs to Tristan. The lovers meet secretly and are betrayed. Marke's poisoned spear fatally wounds Tristan. Isolde, heartbroken, dies at his side.

In the adjoining chapel, the king, who is a firm Catholic, can look up to his idol, Saint Louis, King Louis IX of France.

It is in this very bedroom that Ludwig II experiences his darkest hour. It is here that in the night of 12 June 1886, after having been removed from power, he is declared insane, arrested and dethroned as King of Bavaria.

King Marke surprises Tristan and Isolde in the park

Isolde's love death

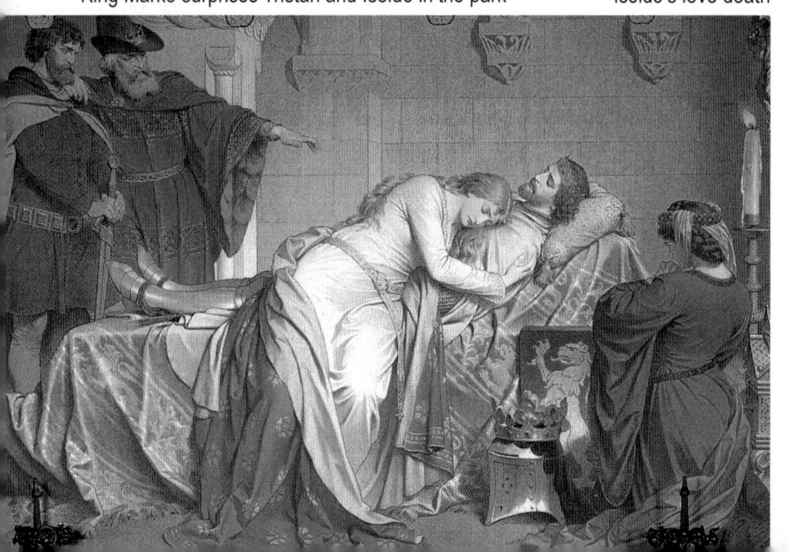

DIE LETZTEN TROSTUNGEN

"Sticherl, guard these rooms like a shrine, do not allow them to be profaned by the curious, as it is here that I had to endure the bitterest hours of my life."

This plea that Ludwig directed toward his valet Stich is in vain – it is only a few weeks after his death that his castles are opened for the public.

The construction of Neuschwanstein stretches over 17 years. Despite this length of time, the palace remains unfinished. Ludwig, who spends a total of 172 days here, only knows his grail castle as a construction site. The completion of the project is continuously deferred due to the king's new ideas and corrections.
And thus the medieval castle as originally planned becomes a castle of the grail. The reasons for this can surely be found in the king's increasing loss of power, his reclusiveness and his struggle to find salvation.

King Ludwig II on the balcony of the throne room

"To escape the tiring aspects of life as well as the tedious court etiquette, Louis XIV had the summer residence of Trianon built in the park of Versailles.
I now wish to have a small residence built at Linderhof, with a garden that is not too large in the style of the Renaissance."

Ludwig II 1868 to court secretary Düfflipp

Chapel and king's country hunting estate at Linderhof

Since his youth, Ludwig, as a nature lover, has been well acquainted with the Graswang Valley near Oberammergau with its rugged mountain peaks. His father had a small country hunting lodge built there.

Between 1868 and 1874, Ludwig has the king's lodge expensively and extravagantly rebuilt.

"Oh, how truly dear and cherished has it become to me, the castle at Linderhof,"

Ludwig notes in his diary

The Palace of Linderhof is the smallest of Ludwig's three castles and the only one that was ever finished. Ludwig particularly loves the 'royal villa' and spends most of his time here during the last years of his life. The palace and the adjoining 50 hectares of park combine Ludwig's various passions: France at the time of the Sun King, the Oriental world and the romantic, knightly world of the sagas of the Middle Ages.

The park grounds, which begin in rigidly stylized arrangements in the French style near the palace, change to an Italian Renaissance terrace and, finally, to an English-style park.

Royal Garden Director Carl von Effner plans these impressive park grounds and gardens. Ludwig is so pleased with his work that he has Effner raised to nobility.

A fountain with the figure of Pheme in gilt zinc by Franz Walker forms the center point of the west ornamental garden. The statues by Johann Nepomuk Hautmann depict the four seasons.

Whereas the statues and bas-reliefs of the facade glorify the Bavarian Monarchy, inside the palace the visitor is welcomed to the world of Louis XIV.

'NEC PLURIBUS IMPAR' – freely translated as 'Superior to Many', is the dictum of the Bourbons and decorates the ceiling of the vestibule. Below is a statue of the Sun King who is so venerated by Ludwig. The statue is a smaller copy of the one which was on display in Paris in 1699.

The vase with Esther in the entrance hall is a gift from Napoleon III. The biblical tale of the beautiful Esther and King Ahasveros is one of Ludwig's favorite themes in drama.

The staircase, which is inspired by the ambassadors' staircase in Versailles, leads to the main rooms.

Palace of Linderhof, vestibule with staircase

Esther vase, Sèvres porcelain

PLURIBUS IMPAR
REGI
RELIGIONIS VINDICI
PATRI PATRIAE

Following the Baroque tradition, the king's apartments can only be entered through one of the two anterooms. These rooms are called 'Gobelin' rooms because of the wall paintings in the style of Gobelin tapestry. The scenes of harmony and love emphasize the character of the palace as a place of retreat.

When the king is in residence, two life-size peacocks made of porcelain stand in front of the palace.
Whether Ludwig, who according to Wagner had no talent for music, ever played the piano harmonium is not known.
The ceiling painting in the east Gobelin chamber symbolizes the movement of the sun with Apollo and Aurora as the rising sun. Together with Apollo, Venus greets the night in the west Gobelin chamber.

The Three Graces in marble

West Gobelin chamber (music room)

"There is only one animal that truly thrills me. Nature's most beautiful creation is the peacock,"

Ludwig notes in his diary

When the king is in residence, two life-size peacocks made of porcelain stand in front of the palace.

East Gobelin chamber

Embroidery on the backrest of a chair

Ludwig II, who in Linderhof wants to live in his fantasy world of the absolute monarchy of Louis XIV, cannot completely disregard his functions and responsibilities as a constitutional monarch. However, the king never grants an audience here in the audience chamber. Ludwig, who is politically well-informed, uses the chamber as a study. Sitting at his throne-like desk, he signs laws, appoints ministers and government officials – degraded to a 'signature machine' as His Majesty is prone to say.
Above him is a canopy whose ermine lining is said to be from the inauguration cloak of his uncle, King Otto of Greece. Behind the desk the Bavarian coat of arms can be seen as well as Bavaria, the patron saint of Bavaria.

Writing utensils with Bavarian coat of arms in the audience chamber

Following French tradition, the main rooms of the palace are connected to one another by four small horseshoe-shaped cabinets. They are all held in a different color and are decorated with oval-shaped pastel portraits. Famous persons from the French court are portrayed here: Louis XV, Marquise de Pompadour, and the Countess Dubarry. The Versailles high society is well-known to Ludwig ll from innumerable plays and books.

The king uses the pink cabinet as a dressing room. He especially enjoys slipping into the court costumes of the French kings.

Blue cabinet, 'Leda and the Swan'

Lilac cabinet, painting: Duchess Marie Anne de Châteauroux, King Louis XV, Marquise de Pompadour

Yellow cabinet, 'Embarkation for Cythera'

Pink cabinet, paintings: Augustin de Maupeou, Countess Dubarry, Duke de Choiseul

King Ludwig II in the dining room next to the 'Tischlein-deck-dich'

The king insists on eating alone. Despite this fact, his servants still have to set the table for at least three or four people. Ludwig believes he is in the company of the French kings, Louis XV and Louis XIV, whose emblem of the sun decorates the cutlery holders. "He sometimes even greets his guests and carries on conversations with them," according to one of the king's cooks.

In order that the king not be disturbed in his fantasies, the dining room is equipped with a 'Tischlein-deck-dich', a table that sets itself. This table, which is a French invention from the 18th century, is set on the lower floor and cranked up to the dining room.

In the last years of his life, Ludwig turns day into night. For the kitchen staff that means that breakfast is served at 5 o'clock in the afternoon, the midday meal at midnight and supper in the morning.

Cutlery holder in the shape of a boat

Ceiling painting in bedchamber, Apollo (with the features of Louis XIV) in a chariot of the sun

As in Versailles, the bedchamber is the central point of the palace and symbolizes the absolute power of the French kings, demonstrated in 'lever', the morning audience, and 'coucher', the evening ceremony.
For this reason, Ludwig has the bedchamber enlarged to 1076 square feet. The chamber also has a ceiling painting – the Ascension of Louis XIV. Here the Sun King is clearly a subject of adoration.

"May God bless me and bless the memory of this great king, Louis XIV,"

Ludwig writes in his diary

Praying chair in bedroom

The bed and royal praying chair are like an altar, separated from the rest of the room by a balustrade.
A chandelier with 108 candles decorates the center of the room.
The rich gold embroidery with ornaments and cherubs, as well as the console tables and the mirror frames of Meissener porcelain all contribute to making the bedchamber the most extravagant room in the palace.
From the window of the bedchamber there is a view of a cascade lined with hedges. The cascade behind the castle is directly lined up to the bedroom and to the Neptune Fountain.

Parts of the original bedroom furniture from Linderhof were handed over to the Bavarian National Museum in 1888 and were on display at the World's Fair in Chicago in 1893. Today this furniture can be seen at the King Ludwig Museum at Herrenchiemsee.

King Ludwig II - Museum, Herrenchiemsee, original bedroom furniture from Linderhof Palace

View from bedroom of cascade and Neptune Fountain

"When residing in the Rococo splendor of my chambers in Linderhof, it is my greatest joy and a never-ending pleasure to immerse myself in the books in which I find such comfort and consolation for so much that is painful and harsh today in this 19th century that I do so despise."

Ludwig II 1874 to his former teacher Miss von Leonrod (nee Meilhaus)

Ludwig, who does not live to see his new bedchamber, uses the hall of mirrors as his bedroom during construction work. The never-ending succession of imaginary rooms, which the hall of mirrors seems to create, gains an additional dimension when considering Ludwig's attempt to escape from his own life into a world of fantasy.

There is hardly any area of the wall that is not covered by a mirror. Following Ludwig's instructions, everything is elaborate and exceedingly valuable: the rosewood desk decorated with gilt bronze fittings and painted porcelain tiles, the centrally heated stoves of lapis lazuli, on which statues made of Carrara marble stand, the small table with an exquisite mosaic of the Bavarian coat of arms made of lapis lazuli, amethyst and chalcedonian quartz.

Absorbed in his reading matter, which usually is of an historical nature, Ludwig, a nocturnal being, often sits under the ivory chandelier, the most valuable piece in the palace.

Niche in the hall of mirrors with ivory chandelier, couch und small table

Hall of mirrors.
On the right, statue of
Louis XV in Carrara
marble

From the hall of mirrors, Ludwig looks out on a carefully composed formal garden with a basin. In the center of the basin, natural water pressure causes a fountain to shoot up 98 feet from a gilded group of figures. Behind the fountain, stairs and paths lead to the terraced garden.
This symmetry is broken only by a 300-year-old linden tree which gives the castle its name. Ludwig has a platform built into the tree's branches which is reached by wooden stairs. He even takes his meals there a couple of times.

When Ludwig climbs the stairs of the garden, he always greets the bust of Queen Marie Antoinette of France by stroking her cheek. This ritual is later used, among others, as evidence of his insanity.

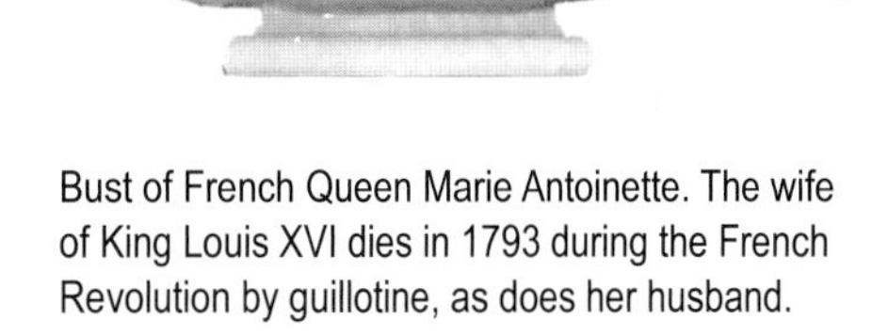

Bust of French Queen Marie Antoinette. The wife of King Louis XVI dies in 1793 during the French Revolution by guillotine, as does her husband.

Ludwig on his platform in the linden tree

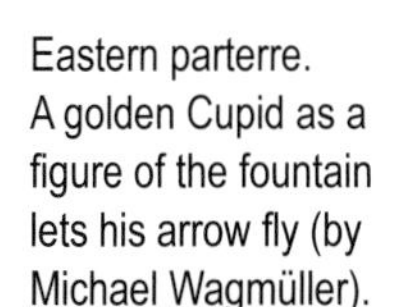

Eastern parterre.
A golden Cupid as a figure of the fountain lets his arrow fly (by Michael Wagmüller).

Statue of Venus with two cupids in the round temple at the top of the terrace gardens

A round temple with the figure of Venus is at the top of the stairs. Venus is often represented in Linderhof. However, neither she nor any other woman plays a role in Ludwig's life.

There is, however, a very special friendship between Ludwig and the Empress Elisabeth of Austria. Sissi is also eccentric, reclusive and shy. One time the unhappy king reveals that Elisabeth is the only woman who might have been able to change him.

Originally a theater is planned instead of the Venus Temple. Ludwig, however, drops these plans. He recognizes that a second large building would endanger the harmony of Linderhof as a total work of art. It is, however, surprising that the king, as a great lover and patron of the theater, does not have a theater built.

Already in 1867, Ludwig wants to give Munich a theater and a boulevard planned by Gottfried Semper. This plan, however, fails due to Munich's bureaucracy. And also because of Wagner who fears that the high cost of the project could endanger his own generous financial support by the king.

During his lifetime, Ludwig attends more than 400 theater performances, 200 of them as private performances. Thus he can dream away undisturbed while watching plays and operas which are mostly of an historical nature.

Elisabeth Empress of Austria, called 'Sissi'

Model by Gottfried Semper of theater planned for Munich. King Ludwig II Museum, Herrenchiemsee

"I cannot fully immerse myself in a play if people are constantly staring at me and following my every move. I want to watch the play and not be an object on display for the masses!"

Ludwig II to actor Ernst Possart.

View from the music pavilion to the north slope of Linderhof Palace, terraced garden and Venus Temple

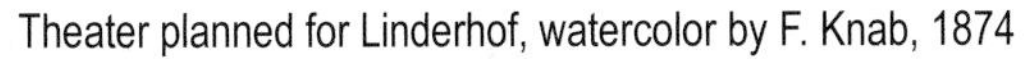

Theater planned for Linderhof, watercolor by F. Knab, 1874

Venus Grotto in the park grounds of Linderhof

Park grounds of Linderhof, entrance to the Venus Grotto

One of the largest stage sets, hardly to be seen from outside, is built in the park of Linderhof.
The king enters the artificial cave made of plaster, steel and concrete through a stone door. The cave is inspired by the Venus Grotto in the mountain, Hörselberg, from Wagner's opera 'Tannhäuser' and the blue grotto of Capri.

King Ludwig II in his sea-shell boat

The cave, which is equipped with a lake, a waterfall, a wave machine, heating system and electrical lighting effects is, for Ludwig, a place of illusion and magic.
In the golden shell-shaped boat, a motive from Lohengrin, Ludwig is rowed about the lake accompanied by two live swans. The colored lights change every ten minutes illuminating the artificial waves, the rocky cliffs and the king drifting along in his golden shell as if lost in a fairy tale.

"I don't want to know how it works, I only want to see the results,"

is what Ludwig says to his technicians, who are having great problems getting the correct blue for the grotto. To get this just right, Ludwig's master of the stables travels twice to Capri in order to study the blue of the cave there.
The electricity for the grotto is generated by 24 dynamos in a building located 650 feet away, making it one of Bavaria's first electric power plants. With the help of modern technology, Ludwig is able to immerse himself even more into his world of fairy tales and sagas.

In 1876, the first year of the Bayreuth Festival, Ludwig has Hunding's Hut built deep in the Ammer Forest. This hut is based on the stage set from Wagner's opera, 'Die Walküre'. The hut was rebuilt on the palace park grounds in 1990.

Here Ludwig sits on bearskin rugs, absorbed in his reading which is in great contrast to his rough surroundings. Or he watches 'tableaux vivants'. At his demand, his servants have to present old German drinking feasts for him to watch.

Park grounds of Linderhof, Hunding's Hut

Moorish Kiosk,
Peacock Throne

To escape the present everyday world and to live out his fantasies of an absolute monarch, Ludwig also flees into the world of the Orient. This special interest in everything that is exotic and oriental he shares with many of his contemporaries.
When visiting the World's Fair in 1867 in Paris, a Moorish kiosk catches Ludwig's eye. More extravagantly built and decorated with rare plants, it is destined to also adorn the park of Linderhof.
The king also commissions an oriental peacock throne decorated with Bohemian glass. In the Orient the peacock stands for royal dignity.
Sitting on a divan covered with silk brocade, Ludwig is served violet punch and enjoys the magical oriental play of light through the stained glass windows.

Park grounds of
Linderhof,
Moorish Kiosk

As soon as the Moorish Kiosk is finished, Ludwig becomes again fascinated by oriental building styles. Thus, in 1878, he buys this wooden pavilion in the style of a Moroccan house at the World Fair in Paris. He has the inside altered according to his wishes. The wooden building was originally put up at the 'Stockalpe' near the Austrian border and has been standing in the park grounds since 1998.

Park grounds of Linderhof, Moroccan House

St. Anne's Chapel

St. Anne's Chapel, built by an abbot of the Ettal Monastery, existed long before the other buildings were put up on the palace grounds. Ludwig has the chapel rebuilt. The new stained glass windows depict the king's patron saint, Saint Ludwig. The deeply religious king regularly attends mass here together with local farmers.

Ludwig uses Linderhof as a retreat and as a starting point for excursions into his imaginary worlds that he has built on and around the park grounds. He is the director, the stage setter and the main character all in one.

And it is here in Linderhof, that he has the horses harnessed to his Rococo sleigh for his legendary nocturnal sleigh rides. Destination is always one of the 14 hunting lodges between Schwangau and Berchtesgaden which he took over from his father.

Ludwig II on a nocturnal sleigh ride in the Ammer Mountains,
R. Wenig 1885

However, it is not the love of hunting that draws him again and again into the mountains but love of nature and the seclusion,

"How I do enjoy staying at my beloved Hohenschwangau. Now, with the light of the full moon it is truly marvelous and so romantic. I often go on sleigh rides and can immerse myself in my books. There is still enough time later to return to that horrible city and feel miserable."

Ludwig II to Baroness Leonrod

"… to feel this bliss in the sublime seclusion of the mountains, far away from 'daylight' that hated enemy, far from the scorching light of day! Far from profane everyday life and political intrigues which want to strangle me and smother all art and beauty in this world."

Ludwig II in July 1871 to Richard Wagner

Already as a young man, Ludwig finds such a spot while on one of his long rides in the high mountains. Near Partenkirchen, at an altitude of almost 6500 feet, Ludwig has a mountain lodge built on Schachen Alp in 1870. This lodge can only be reached after a hike of several hours.
Even in this very Bavarian mountain idyll, Ludwig is still fascinated by exotic cultures. Surprisingly, the remote mountain lodge has a 'Turkish Hall' on the top floor in the style of a sultan's palace in Istanbul. And it is also here that one can find the king reading, dressed in traditional Turk-

Living room on the ground floor

Turkish Hall on the top floor

ish attire. His servants, also in Turkish attire, sit on carpets and pillows.
The rooms on the lower floor have traditional Swiss pine paneling and are plainly decorated in the style of a Bavarian lodge. Ludwig always visits Schachen on his birthday on 25 August where there is a large fireworks display in his honor.

"As in a wonderful dream I think back to my travels to France, and to my cherished Versailles which I could then finally behold."

Ludwig II 1874 to Count von Dürckheim

Palace of Versailles, painting in the first antechamber in the Palace of Herrenchiemsee

The palace of Herrenchiemsee is meant to give particularly impressive testimony to Ludwig's idealization of the French Bourbon kings and will be by far his most expensive project.

Already in his early years, Ludwig shows great interest in France and the Sun King, Louis XIV.
The Bavarian king has the court architect Dollman draw up blueprints, 13 in all, for a palace based on Versailles. However, the site at Linderhof does not offer enough room for the king's requirements. Thus, the project with the code name 'Meicost Ettal' is moved to the Herreninsel Island in Lake Chiemsee. 'Meicost Ettal' is an anagram for the letters in the famous quote from Louis XIV, "L'État, c'est moi." – "I am the state."

"His Majesty can not endure it that this palace is built at Chiemsee and not at Linderhof. Art itself will have to make this unpleasant state of affairs pleasant and help us to forget the area and the lake."
The only thing that Ludwig, becoming even more shy and lonely, appreciates about this location is the remoteness of the island.

The foundation stone is laid in 1878. Karl von Effner plans a park to go along with the main facade, which is an exact replica of the main facade of Versailles. As in Versailles, a Latona fountain is placed in the center of the park.

Palace of Herrenchiemsee, garden façade, west front

Fortuna Fountain

Latona, one of Zeus' mistresses, flees with her children Artemis and Apollo to a village. As the villagers do not allow the mother and children to quench their thirst in a lake, they are turned into frogs – as to be seen on the tiers of the fountain.
In 1874 Ludwig visits Versailles where the fountains are turned on in honor of his birthday. The cost of this event adds up to the enormous sum of 50,000 francs.

"Not as a copy but as in the spirit of Louis XIV,"

– such are the stipulations for this building project. Ludwig II has the large side fountains of Versailles duplicated, the figures of Pheme and Fortuna however are copied from the park of the Spanish palace San Ildefonso.
The Palace of Herrenchiemsee with all of its park grounds should not be seen as a strict replica of Versailles but as a building in the historicist style.

The king enters his palace through the marble court. In Versailles this court is on the front side of the palace which faces the city.

Pheme Fountain

Marble court, east side

A pair of peacocks made of enameled bronze dominates the vestibule on the ground floor.

The magnificence of the palace can already be seen in the south staircase which is a replica of the ambassadors' staircase of Versailles during the reign of the Sun King. As this staircase was demolished in 1752, Ludwig has his staircase reconstructed according to old sketches.
The glass ceiling, which is an invention of the 19th century, completely changes the character of the staircase. The colors are more intensive, a sight that is not for the king's eyes as Ludwig, who sleeps during the day, only visits his palace during the night by candlelight. When he is present the staircase is decorated with thousands of roses and lilies.
Whereas in Versailles a bust of Louis XIV greeted the nobility, Apollo, god of the sun, and Diana, goddess of the moon, are placed in the staircase. They emphasize the symbolism of day and night in the palace.

State staircase, Diana with two nymphs, statue in the niche on the landing

The way to the state bedchamber begins in the royal guard room. It corresponds to the 'Salle des Gardes' in that the halberds of the royal guards are lined up between the windows. The busts are of French marshals.
The paintings depict the Sun King's military campaigns and activities of war, the ceiling painting, the triumph of Mars.

Hall of the royal guards

Baptism of the Duke of Burgundy

As the original furnishings in Versailles were largely lost during the French Revolution, Ludwig and his architects have to undertake extensive research on the original furnishings in Versailles.

The splendid cabinet in the first antechamber was not completed and was probably meant to be used for musical instruments.

Ludwig is linked to the Bourbons by a line of godfathers. Ludwig's godfather is also his grandfather, Ludwig I, whose godfather in turn is Louis XVI of France. Ludwig sees himself thus in direct line to the French kings, who reach back to Louis IX who was canonized. The Bourbon kings who have the same name as he does become objects of glorification and adoration.

The 'Salon de l'Oeil de Boeuf', also known as the 'Ox Eye Room' because of its oval windows, was the room where the princes were christened in Versailles. Ludwig has his room built much larger than the one in Versailles.

The ceiling painting, an allegory of Aurora, goddess of dawn, glorifies day and night. Astraeus in the blue cloak of night, followed by Chronus, tries to evade Aurora, who is heralded by Mercury.

The room is dominated by a statue of the King of France, Louis XIV, who is riding a rearing horse. Here one of Ludwig's favorite mounts was used as a model. The scepter points the way to the center of the palace, the state bedchamber.

First antechamber

Second antechamber, ceiling painting with Aurora und Astraeus

The state bedchamber is the spiritual core for Ludwig's Herrenchiemsee.
Here, in his own Versailles, the Bavarian king can live his dream of an absolute monarchy. A dream, however, for which he was born two centuries too late.

As homage to the Sun King, the state bedchamber has an incomparable décor. The exquisite textiles were commissioned already three years before the foundation stone was even laid.

Bronze equestrian statue of Louis XIV of France

"This is a 'monument', not to be used, but rather for 'contemplation'. It is meant to become a temple of fame, so to speak, where I can commemorate the memory of Louis XIV." Ludwig II to his court secretary Düfflipp

The material alone for the canopy of the gilded ceremonial bed, where in Versailles 'lever' and 'coucher' took place, is seven years in the making. The canopy far excels the one in Versailles.
'Apollo with sun chariot' in the ceiling painting was first painted with Ludwig's features but had to be repainted with those of the Sun King.

Second antechamber, called 'Ox Eye Room'

Audience Louis XIV in his bedchamber in Versailles.

Ceiling painting in the royal bedchamber, Apollo with sun chariot

The royal bed-chamber was the first completed room in the Palace of Herrenchiemsee to be presented to the king in September 1881.

To be true to Versailles, Ludwig orders,

"Everything that is Bavarian must be removed from Chiemsee."

The same is true for the council chamber where Ludwig certainly does not want to see any Bavarian flags, lions or other Bavarian symbols. A magnificent painting of Louis XIV is surrounded by candelabra as an object for devotion.

The exquisite clocks in the council chamber are the work of Carl Schweizer, clockmaker from Munich, and are replicas of those in Versailles.
Ludwig loves to look at complex and sophisticated clockwork.

"If my life was not regulated like clockwork, I would not be able to endure the loneliness which weighs so heavily upon me but with which I cannot do without."

In the ceiling painting, in line with the significance of the chamber, Mercury brings the king divine advice.

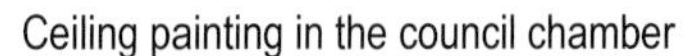

Ceiling painting in the council chamber

Council chamber,
clock with inlaid rosewood

Louis XIV of France, ceiling painting in the Great Hall of Mirrors

"You know that the great hall of mirrors and the two accompanying chambers have to be exact replicas of those in Versailles. An apparent magnificence is not enough to reflect the magnificence of that extraordinary and wonderful epoch,"

Ludwig II to his court secretary Düfflipp

Thus, Ludwig's Great Hall of Mirrors is 26 feet longer than the original.
Ludwig's architects, artisans and painters spend much time in Paris in order to carefully study the original. If this is not sufficient, the court photographer is also commissioned. Ludwig himself also carefully studies the plans. Being a demanding and exacting individual, he continuously corrects and contributes to the plans and sketches.

Great Hall of Mirrors illuminated at night by 2188 candles

The paintings in the Great Hall of Mirrors glorify important deeds in the life of Louis XIV.
The 'Galerie des Glaces' is an optical masterpiece. On the one side, 17 arched windows set between red pilasters open to the park. On the other side of the hall, mirrors are set opposite the windows so that the view of the park is reflected in them.
The furnishings, which are no longer in Versailles, are reconstructed according to historical records. This includes marble busts of Roman emperors, gilded vases for orange trees as well as 44 candelabra.

When King William I of Prussia is proclaimed German Emperor in 1871 in this very hall in Versailles, all of German aristocracy is present. Only one is missing – Ludwig II of Bavaria. He views this event with great disfavor. Ludwig, for whom the independence of the Bavarian crown has always been of the utmost importance, becomes, with this act, a vassal of Prussia. For the king personally this is surely his greatest political defeat.

Hall of War, left.
Hall of Peace, right.

The smaller chambers at either end of the Great Hall of Mirrors, the Hall of War and the Hall of Peace, are entered through doors which are shaped like an arch of triumph. Thus, these three rooms take up the full width of the palace which is 330 feet.

In 1882, the completed state rooms are turned over to the impatiently waiting king. Ludwig himself usually only visits Herrenchiemsee once a year in the fall. Whereas the French kings held great festivities in the hall of mirrors in Versailles, Ludwig always visits the 'Galerie des Glaces' alone and only by night. Lit by 2188 candles, the hall is turned into a magical dream world for Ludwig alone. The reclusive king never had any intention of receiving guests here.

Artemis, statue in a niche in the Great Hall of Mirrors

Great Hall of Mirrors

Whereas red is the main color for the state bedchamber, Ludwig's bedroom is kept in his favorite color – blue as symbol for the king of the night.

The bed with figures of Venus and Adonis is richly adorned with embroidery. The tapestry depicts the triumph of Louis XIV over vice. Along with the dove on the canopy as a symbol of the Holy Ghost, this refers to Ludwig's lifelong struggle for salvation.

The blue sphere in the center of the room is worth noting. When this 'moon' is illuminated, it fills the bedroom with an evenly distributed blue light. The 'Royal Illuminator' experiments – as in the grotto in Linderhof – one and a half years – and this only to achieve the right blue hue of the sphere. Only after innumerable trials and demonstrations does he receive the king's approval.
However, Ludwig resides only once in this, his last castle, and can enjoy this magical moment only for nine nights.

Venus at the forge of Vulcan, ceiling fresco in bathroom

A hidden door in the bedroom serves the king as an entrance to the dressing room and to the bathroom.
The oval-shaped pool is decorated with a panorama which depicts the birth of Venus. It takes a total of eight hours for the pool to be filled with warm water. The supporting construction of the pool is made of steel and stands witness to Ludwig's great interest in modern technology.

The dressing room is next to the bathroom and is lavishly decorated with innumerable mirrors. This mirrored dressing room is typical for castles built in the 19th century in southern Germany. Ludwig chooses the same fashionable style for the blue salon.

Neptune und Amphitrite, ceiling painting in dressing room

A splendid mantelpiece made of Meissener porcelain is especially notable in the blue salon.
The mirrors, which are framed by carvings of branches and foliage, create an illusion of endlessness. Furthermore, the carvings on the walls are continued in the stucco on the ceiling.

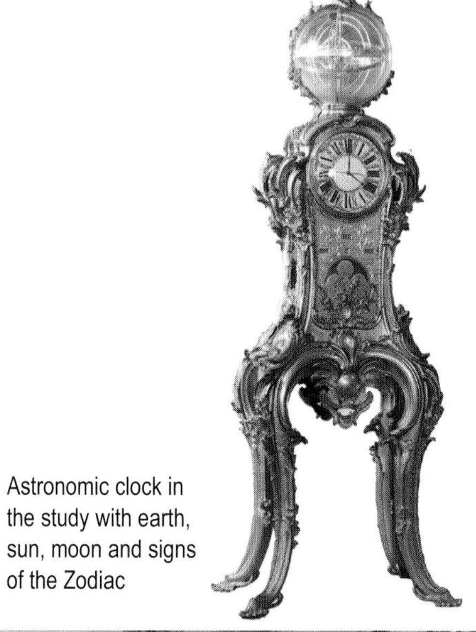

Astronomic clock in the study with earth, sun, moon and signs of the Zodiac

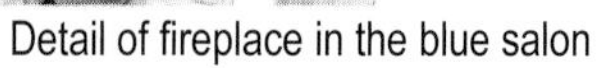

Detail of fireplace in the blue salon

The most spectacular object in the study is the large roll-top desk which stands in front of the portrait of Louis XV. It was made in Paris and is a copy of the famous 'Bureau du Roi' in Versailles. Ludwig has the king's insignia, which were removed during the French Revolution, reconstructed exactly as on the original.

Elephant clock in the study

Bust of Madame de Pompadour in the dining room

Ludwig also prefers to take his meals alone here. As in Linderhof, a 'Tischlein-deck-dich' (a table that sets itself) fulfils this wish. The table is set for meals on the floor below and then is cranked up to the dining room.

The king does not wish to see servants or profane guests in his dining room. He wishes to have only the presence of his

Lifting device of the 'Tischlein-deck-dich' under the dining room

'French guests' – in the form of busts of Louis XV and Madame de Pompadour.
Ludwig's private living quarters are not based on Versailles. Here he has chosen to be inspired by other sources – for the dining room, for example, by a salon in the Hotel de Soubise in Paris
The flowers on the table are life-like replicas in paper-thin Meissener porcelain.

The dining room is dominated by a porcelain chandelier with 108 candles. This is the heaviest and most valuable piece that has ever been produced by the famous Meissener porcelain manufacturer. According to instructions by the king, all plans and moulds for this masterpiece have to be destroyed so that it is impossible to copy it.

Detail of porcelain chandelier in dining room

Small gallery.
As in the hall of mirrors, the small gallery next to the dining hall has two corner rooms such as those in the 'Petite Galerie' in Versailles.

Portrait of Ludwig II on a medallion over the door.

The adjoining room – the Oval Porcelain Room – is created completely in porcelain. The detailed designs on the console tables, vases and chandeliers and even the frame of the mirror over the mantelpiece are made of this fragile material.

Even the massive desk of rosewood is decorated with painted porcelain tiles.

Surprisingly, on one of the doors there is a medallion of the king. It is the only portrait of Ludwig II in the palace. This has to be something that the painter did on his own, as the King would never have allowed it. This was, however, no problem, as the doors were delivered after the king's death.

The king is seen here in his younger years. Ludwig is, as a young man, much loved by his people for his handsomeness. However, he loses his teeth when he is quite young due to overindulgence in sweets. In just a few years, the Adonis-like king becomes a man who weighs 280 pounds and suffers from various physical ailments. His appearance only makes him more of a recluse. He finds solace in the excessive consumption of alcohol.

The political situation also affects Ludwig's emotional frame of mind. Degraded as a Bavarian monarch to being a vassal of Prussia, the building projects have long become his raison d'ètre. The king gives thousands of instructions for the furnishing of his castles. He researches, selects, designs and controls all projects. This is truly a remarkable workload as he has several projects going on at the same time. Ludwig finds talented architects and craftsmen whom he spurs on to top performance.

King Ludwig II, photographer Joseph Albert, 1884

The way to the north staircase is like waking from a dream. Huge walls of red brick are evidence of the incompleteness of the king's dreams and give the impression of a stage set.

Ludwig himself does not want to see this side of the palace. When he enters the construction site to inspect the finished rooms, canvases are hung and wooden and plaster furniture is placed in the rooms.

The north wing, though almost completed, is torn down after the king's death. Only the main wing can be seen today in all its magnificence.

Unfinished north staircase in the Palace of Herrenchiemsee

Palace of Herrenchiemsee, to the left, the north wing which was pulled down after the king's death. Historical photo, 1888

Finally, the enormous amount of construction work and the king's never-ending outpouring of new ideas clearly begin to reach financial limits. Ludwig finances his projects solely from his private funds. Despite these massive financial problems, he plans further projects: the castle at Falkenstein, a Chinese summer palace and a Byzantine castle.

First draft of the castle at Falkenstein, Christian Jank, 1883

Shortly after Ludwig moves into his royal apartment in September 1885, he faces insolvency. Most of the construction work has to be stopped. His cabinet refuses to supply him with additional funds. Foreign banks even threaten foreclosure. Desperate, Ludwig writes to his secretary of the cabinet,

"Since the interruption of the building projects, which are so infinitely important to me, I have lost my only joy. I therefore urge you to do everything possible to make my ardent wishes come true. You would thus give me a new chance in life."

In the end, Herrenchiemsee costs 16 million marks, more than Linderhof at 8.5 million marks and Neuschwanstein at 6 million marks together.

Ludwig has a yearly income of about 4 million marks. From this he finances his court, generously supporting Richard Wagner and the Bayreuth Festival as well as granting enormous sums of money to theaters in Munich. In addition there are generous gifts to, for example, his gardener, other members of the royal family or favored actors.

In 1886 Ludwig's debts have increased to 14 million marks. The royal family sees the reputation of the monarchy in danger. His ministers are afraid of being made responsible for this calamity and are worried about losing their positions. Due to the considerable building activity and the king's withdrawal from public life, it is said by some that they believe they see signs of insanity. It becomes evident in 1875 that Otto, the king's brother, is mentally ill. It is therefore suspected that the king has the same unfortunate hereditary disease.

Thus is the fateful decision made to declare the king insane. An official document to this end based on questions to servants and circumstantial evidence is quickly put together. Its scientific value is, however, more than doubtful.

Ludwig's uncle Luitpold becomes prince regent after the king's death

Bismarck, who corresponds with Ludwig, thinks very highly of the Bavarian monarch. He supports him throughout the years with a sum of about 5 million marks. And he finally advises the king in his hopeless situation, "Your Majesty should return to Munich, show yourself to the people and present your interests to Parliament."

Ludwig, however, caught in his world of dreams and loneliness brought on by himself, no longer has the strength to do so.

German Chancellor Otto von Bismarck

Ludwig's Brother, Prince Otto

Dr. Bernhard von Gudden, Professor of Psychiatry

"I cannot, no I cannot, I can no longer endure being stared at by thousands of people."

It is thus that Ludwig II finally experiences his darkest hour in his bedroom in Neuschwanstein. A commission headed by Dr. Bernhard von Gudden informs him during the night of 12 June 1886 of his dethronement.

"There is no need to make a statement to the people regarding Your Majesty's current situation. Your Majesty's mental capacities are already of such a nature that there is a total lack of insight on Your Majesty's part, a wide discrepancy between thinking and reality as well as an inability to act by free will. Your Majesty believes himself to be endowed with absolute power and has, by self-induced isolation, become a recluse and stands like a blind man, without a guide, close to the abyss." Stunned, Ludwig answers,

"How can you possibly declare me to be insane when you haven't even examined me?"

And it is true that there never was an examination nor were his two personal physicians heard in this matter.

Dr. Johann von Lutz, Head of the Cabinet, commissions the official report on Ludwig II.

Ludwig II., photograph 1885

"I could endure it if they took the crown away from me, but it would be the death of me to be declared insane… I could not bear to have the same fate as my brother Otto."

After his dethronement, the king is taken that very night to the Castle of Berg south of Munich. Ludwig and Dr. von Gudden never return from a walk taken the next day. Both are found dead in the shallow waters of Lake Starnberg. Officially, the cause of death is by drowning. However,

Ludwig II lying in state in the court chapel

many doubt this official version. The real circumstances that led to the King's death in the lake remain up to today a mystery.

The statesman Bismarck writes about Ludwig in his memoirs, "The people of the world will most certainly change their verdict about King Ludwig when they not only admire his artistic creations, but also take a look at his correspondence in matters of state. One cannot confirm a death sentence by using notes that his servants found in waste baskets and elsewhere and which his ministers used as evidence against him. I shall honor him with the greatest respect in my memoirs".

When his building projects were stopped, King Ludwig II lost all reason to live. Today, we stand fascinated before the legacy of the Bavarian monarch: Neuschwanstein, Linderhof and Herrenchiemsee – contrasting worlds to the reality of the 19th century which he so much despised. It was a difficult time for Ludwig to be king at this turning point in history.
The dreams of a lonely and deeply unhappy man were transformed into brick, built in the hope of finding personal salvation, but to no avail.

Memorial cross in Lake Starnberg

"I am simply of another mind than most of my countrymen… and so must I endure that I am laughed at, despised and slandered. They call me a fool. Will God, when He summons me to Him, also call me a fool?"

Ludwig 1882 to author Lew Vanderpoole

Furniture from the living quarters of Ludwig II in the Munich Residence

The King Ludwig II Museum was re-opened in the Royal Palace of Herrenchiemsee in 1987. The life and the tragic, early death of the Bavarian monarch are documented by memorabilia exhibited in 12 especially refurnished rooms in the palace. Treasures such as Ludwig's christening gown, his coronation robe, two decorative cloaks for the planned wedding of Ludwig with Sophie, Duchess in Bavaria, the king's death mask as well as numerous portraits and works of art can be seen. The exhibition also deals with Ludwig's influence on the applied arts, theater and music of his time. Ludwig's long lasting friendship with Richard Wagner is documented by portraits, examples of music scores and models of stage sets.

The museum also focuses on Ludwig himself, the man who commissioned such magnificent buildings. His three royal castles, Herrenchiemsee, Linderhof and Neuschwanstein, are represented by special objects of art. There is a room especially reserved for the original furniture from the first bedroom in the Castle of Linderhof. The royal bed had already been displayed at the German Exhibition of Applied Arts in Munich in 1888 and again at the World's Fair in Chicago in 1893.

Christening robe of Ludwig II

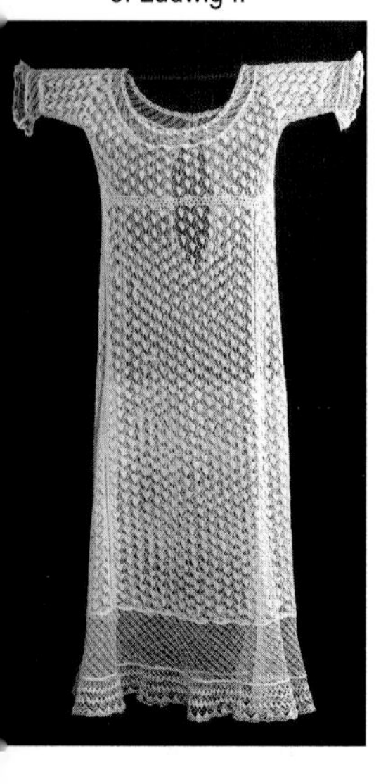

Model of the Apollo Fountain in Herrenchiemsee

Furniture from the audience chamber of the Munich Residence

When he was a young crown prince, Ludwig had his own apartment furnished in the Münchner Residenz (Munich Royal Residence) in 1863. Although the apartment was destroyed during World War II, parts of the splendid furnishings were saved. The king's audience chamber from the Munich Royal Residence can be seen at the museum. It was the king's wish that the new furnishings of the rooms be based on the magnificent style of King Louis XIV of France. Furthermore, the king had a winter garden built on the roof of the Munich Royal Residence. This self-supporting construction which weighed tons was finished in 1872. However, it was torn down after Ludwig's death. The winter garden, which seemed to have been inspired by a fairy tale, housed, among other things, a variety of tropical plants, a grotto, an oriental gazebo as well as a lake with swans. The original boat from the lake can be seen in the museum.

Winter garden on the roof of the Munich Residence

Photographs were taken with the kind permission of the Bavarian Department of State-owned Palaces, Gardens and Lakes in Munich and the Wittelsbacher Compensation Fund.

All photographs were taken by Wilhelm and Klaus Kienberger with the exception of the following:
Bavarian Department of State-owned Palaces, Gardens and Lakes, Munich: pages 94 and 95; Lothar Cornely: bottom of cover and page 97

The historical photographs and drawings are from the archives of the Bavarian Department of State-owned Palaces, Gardens and Lakes; the community of Schwangau; Otto-von-Bismarck Foundation, Friedrichsruh.

Text: Klaus Kienberger
Editor: Petra Scheibenbogen
Image editing, layout and typesetting:
Wilhelm Kienberger Ltd, Lechbruck, Germany

Printed in Germany

Wilhelm Kienberger Ltd
Flösserstrasse 2
D-86983 Lechbruck
Tel: 0049 (0) 8862 8236
Fax: 0049 (0) 8862 7407
E-Mail: info@kienberger.com

Translated from the German by Bonny Schmid-Burleson

ISBN: 978-3-933638-66-3